Water Rising

Tessa Triest

BookLeaf
Publishing

India | USA | UK

Dedication

I dedicate these poems to my family.

My artistic father, my innovative mother, my courageous sister, and my force of nature husband. He is excellent at anything and everything he does.

Thank you for answering my anxious calls throughout all of my years of school, and for being the loving, caring family that you are.

Preface

There is something about water that scares me,
the tendrils of endless weight,
that can pound on your lungs.
The icy smiles before they break and fall apart.
The beauty. The lure. The blanket of movement.
I want to be under that pure contradiction.

Acknowledgements

I would like to acknowledge all of my writing buddies throughout college and high school, my professors, and especially my best friend Taylor for reading through my 3am poems and editing them with me.

1. Buried in Paint

When I die bury me in your favorite flavor of paint.

I want to be earth-bound and water-based,

like the sirens binding men to rocks, screwing them until

their lives are but the sound of the waves crashing along

their jawbones.

I want the paint to seep into my pores and fill my

crevices, so that my pale body becomes colorful again.

Perhaps I lived a full life, but I want to be so pretty when

I'm dead that the old enlightenment folk write poetry

about me and my Frankenstein-esque beauty.

I felt meaningless in life A and would like to at least

bring technicolor to the roots of the plants around my

grave.

To dream of life growing above me, above all, to

continue on

in some way, or another.

I want my toes to have ombré as the shades of your

favorite colors migrate down my legs, and I want to have

hues of you twinkling on my forehead.

I might be stuck now, but forever growing, older and

more decayed, but oh so pretty like the slowly rotting

shipwreck at the bottom of the ocean.

So mysteriously magnificent,

when a grave robber opens my casket, they need their

sunglasses to rip my body from the ground.

If life was meaningless, might as well make death
worthwhile.

Remember to pour the water in first and then – no
paintbrush needed – just drop it in. The paint.

Fill

me

up.

2. Ikelos Not I

I'm convinced now more than ever that there is no way
to survive such an insipid, tumultuous journey.
What once was an intrepid runner,
deflecting every chaos
every energy—it has become a nightmare.
Dreams are what we want now more than ever.
Dreams that suck at the nape of our necks
until that precious skin,
pale and porcelain, resembles a mossy pond, green and
splotchy.
There are butterflies there, touching ground, wings
sinking into muck...
They, the reality people, tell me that I can't dream
forever, "Nothing would be real."
"You would never exist."
To see yourself and not you at all. That is not existence.
Everything is through the vision of our own two
interesting eyes. Eyes powered by brain.
Through which we want to see we will see,
a memory sourced from knowledge, books and
photographs,
images of what we denote as identity – who we thought
we were. When the mind forgets, we are no longer.
To take a person's memories and let them keep their

body is murder, a prior-less person is nothing but dead
already.
Some gods could have fooled me,
when inchworms got two sets of no-eyes
Can be torn apart and survive,
writhe through that meaningless dirt and somehow
without struggle, keep on writhing. They do not have to
view what brings them such pain.
Such a pity we beasts do not procure such power,
such immense talent so
through our set of two: vision oracles,
we drink up surrounding nightmare and spit out colorful
vomit
Eat up, young Demi—mommy's gone crazy!
We will never be like worms. They will feed on us.
Damned,
and until cortical existence— where we meet again.

3. Tsunamis As Sheep

When I'm mentally unwell, I dream about Tsunamis.
    The tsunamis hopped around in my head and sucked the air out of me.
    What Tsunamis?
My roommate was waking up to go to morning swim practice. More water.
She could swim.
She violently coughed towards me.
    Am I still sleeping?
    Is she choking from the Tsunami?
 I couldn't make the connection between consciousness and unconsciousness.
The radiator popped while it tirelessly attempted to heat our dorm room.
I shook again.
It was hot.
My pajamas were soaked in sweat.

There is something about water that scares me,
the tendrils of endless weight,
that can pound on your lungs.
The icy smiles before they break and fall apart.
The beauty. The lure. The blanket of movement.
I want to be under that pure contradiction. Sometimes I

wonder if I'd be sad to die under the sea. I wonder if that would be the perfect way to die: floating, nothing but blue above me and green below me. I think of the light reflecting into a pool while I'm holding my breath standing at the bottom of the deep end. There's a beam of reflecting light, broken into different lines, rippling above me. I want to stay under the water, where it's quiet and no one bothers me. I can see figures walking around the pool; their shapes are distorted and colorful. I don't feel obligated to say, "hello," or wave. They understand that I'm unavailable—I'm under water.

Aimless thoughts flooding onto shore like the man o' wars and seashells do after every little movement by the moaning monster.

    My pillow is wet, and my blankets are wrapped tightly around me.
    Above me there's an unimaginable force drowning me,
    but nothing drips; there is no wash of water, sweat.
    Sweat envelops me.
    I think about water constantly.

Images of tsunamis flash before my eyes as I lay in bed,

I count them like sheep, one violent wave crashing over the other.

4. The Conveyer

I am on a thoughtless conveyer
Though I am the thought conveyer.

Up and down, side to side.
My eyes blink with recognition, my lips perk with forced
enthusiasm.

Painted fingers press the "down" button and my robotic
body falls to a new level.

Something I said must have hurt her.

Maybe I didn't validate her feelings enough.

I stare in wandering curiosity, *what will she say next?*

The conveyer stops.

"Is the session over already?"

"Unfortunately, our time is up for today, remember that
if you need anything after hours to call the emergency
hotline. 988."

My head lays vacant while an **out of order sign** sweeps over my eyes.

While I wait for the next patient, I feel my supervisor put old-but newer than before-batteries in my back...

Startup

As I slowly begin to work again, the bell rings and I'm brought up a level.

In walks a small man bundled in a sweatshirt.

Eyes.
Up down.
Side to side.
Smile.
Enthusiasm, but not too much,   he seems sad.

"How are you doing today?"

"Not so good. I feel like I'm living the same day every day."

"I'm sorry. That sounds monotonous. Let's talk about it."

As the sessions wind to an end, the conveyer spits my

body out onto the 11th floor of the parking garage.

The air breathes life into me.

"When getting off the thoughtless conveyer, please
watch your arms and legs. Put used batteries in basket to
retrieve in the morning."

I take my batteries out and step toward my car. 6:37pm.
If life is a constant conveyer, I want off.

The paint on the road home forms one jagged line.
Imperfections are perfect.

5. Women as Tulips

Heavy handed hose crushing flowers
A misty shower is "what many women can handle,
there's too much power in a hard jetted head."
This is when I gained my backbone.
In the shower wondering why my skin was sprouting
splotchy red marks as the beads slammed into me.

Petals crush under pressure, I will no longer.

Though my exterior is bright pink like the two-week
lasting tulips,

My mind will work on turning a new shade: green.
A color of power.

Green signifies strength.
Stems and leaves that will not collapse from the stormy
summer rains.

6. Butterflies Don't Run

From a former collegiate runner being medically forced to quit running.

What did my body go through?
This metamorphosis of degeneration.

I used to wake up in the morning with the knowledge of
the run, the sweaty breaths that would fuel my
antidepressant energy.

A step-by-step process no longer applies because
one step feels
like thirty
and my oxygen
that used to feed the pipes to breathe feels smoky, even
though the air quality is finally back to normal levels.

My back aches and my legs are full of prickly arrows
shooting off every thirty seconds.

The smell of the air is still as beautiful as it was before,
and my eyes still watch the trees flutter by as I push my
heavy body down the sidewalk.

My mind still functions as it used to, an existence made
to move.
To swing my arms and dance to the cadence of my
Brooks running shoes hitting the pavement.

I wonder if when I went through this metamorphosis,
the reason I no longer feel natural running, is because I
now have wings and I'm supposed to fly instead,

For butterflies don't run, they fly.

7. Holding My Tongue and Giving Her My Hand

I've become accustomed to answering with
"I'm sorry."
I'm sorry for the things I've done
I'm sorry for the things I've said
I'm sorry for the things I think
I'm sorry for being me.

But I am also sorry that you have to go through your life
circumstances
and I wrote you yesterday apologizing for your stomach
pains that gripped your night...

I'm sorry for the pain you've felt and I wish I could take
it all away.
I'm sorry for the tears you cry and the fake smiles you
give me when your world feels tired.

I say I'm sorry so much the word itself has lost its
meaning.

Sorry like the bird chirping at my window at sunrise.
Sorry like the egg that cracked on the way home from
the grocery.

Sorry like a cliche waterfall.
Sorry like my grandmother's funeral.

Sorry that when I say the word sorry, I feel so bad that I
can't understand the sorry,

that it becomes sorr-ow instead.

I am sorrowful.
I feel all the sorry's.
I carry them with me and throw them up in the air,
poker chips I've won and never planned on sharing.

Sorry like a dollar bill.
Sorry like a dog's bark.

Sorry doesn't mean much to me anymore, and I
apologize.

I'm sorry for that.

But I will hold my tongue, and say sorry again.

I'm sorry for that too.

8. Right to Left

in Boxed
slightly Tired
cold Bitter
chattering Teeth

summer Gone
.again Never

sockets Frozen

.stuck Trees

9. Night Dance

Another sun-soaked night-dance,
once again becoming bait.
Crickets surfing in the moon-held light.
Drink up worms while the dry-air awaits.
Suck on peppered trees, feel their height.

Dream into a bush, soft whispers of birds singing hate.
Unknown bright smiles prepositioned fight, yellow eyes
through the dark night.
Ruffled grass, bumpy rumbles-movement under metal
gates
People aren't allowed here, restrictions tight.

Sitting on a path that cannot be erased: sealed fate
Instigated memories seep through frog tongues, revealed
croaks of secret
rambunctious nocturnal guffawing hitting rocks and
amplifying water.
No sleep tonight.

Morning is far away, the owls are still dating
The little turtle is coming out of his shell and glancing at
illuminations on the water.
Lily pads begin to sound like percussions against the

pond as the flies bounce their bodies.

The party of the dark.

Notes heard only before day break.

10. After Detroit 1979

While looking at a photograph titled, After Detroit 1979
by Glenn Triest

What about her black satchel made her look down into
the previously rioted streets
white lines dividing the future for her children and the
past
she so righteously remembers
Man—

holes
are not something she care about anymore, graying sepia
tones clouding her inner
sickness,
filtering through her nose, she must carry her weight
through the only coat she owns.

People assume she is penniless,
insignificant into the darkening rained on streets
she has a family at home
two baby girls—
she looks down on herself to find them
after such a day,
doctor told her to wear a mask so that people wouldn't

see contagion

she thinks that is all they will see anyways
she hides herself away
beautiful brown coils pushed up toward her jewel
earring-adorned ears
smooth sundown skin

her brown paper bag holds her reputation
could she hold diapers for her girls?
sandwiches from the local deli?
toilet paper to clean herself and the running, water,
pouring,
consistently from her dreams she never wakes from?
Alcohol flowing through her veins, she's withdrawing
because of work
needs a fix, doesn't want people to know what she
bought?

From all of this the photographer catches her uniqueness
and snaps what he thinks is candid.
She knows he's watching her,
knows everyone is watching her,
with judgement,
hatred.
At least this is her impression.

She left a wonderful impression on the photographer,
but he did not photograph just her,
the atmosphere:
she is Detroit

she does not think so.

11. Last Night I Dreamed I Had Children

Last night I dreamed I had a child.
No one believed me when I told them I was pregnant.
I started to believe I wasn't pregnant.

I went to the hospiital and asked them to re-check.

The nurse told me to lie down because I was in labor.
Labor felt like being full of hot water, steam protruding out of me
droplets falling down my face felt like burning iron.

How could I spend nearly nine months without any preparation?

I called my friends and they told me they were busy and weren't going to make it to the hospital.
I expected it.

The doctor told me I was having a girl,
her heartbeat 142
142 reasons to live.
I decided I'd name her Fiona.

There were no contractions,
unless contractions felt like severe menstrual pain,
squeezing,
fear,
panic,
pain.

I pushed until I felt her being pulled out of me, I worried
they were pulling too hard.
She was deformed, and a he.
I wondered if it was the doctors fault or if my ineptitude
as a mother superstitiously caused it.

I remember looking down and wondering if there was a
way to put him together right,
but he didn't look alive.
His eyes were dull and gray.
Where was the life to him?

An unimaginable sadness overtook me.
I looked for any bit of reality to take hold.
Some reassurance.

The doctor told me to push again,
this time a healthy baby boy was being washed and held
to give to me.

They put his tiny body in my arms and I didn't need
anyone else.
I didn't look around but right at him.
Into his little blue eyes.

Sometimes the world gives you a little piece of yourself
and when you're alone,
you'll look into his eyes and see everything you ever
liked about yourself.

But you'll love him even more.

12. Let Me Be an Orchestra

Swing with me Coffee Bean,
Groove to the rhythm you give me.

Beat, beat, beat.

It doesn't matter that you jingle me a little
too high,
a little too out of pitch,
squeezing me into
some tight
mouth
piece
tightening the aperture on my drowsy
inconsistencies.

Tune me a little nicer,
play me a little more polite.
I don't sing for anyone, just for you my dear.

Scoot on over so the violin can show
you my true sadness
the bari-sax can show you
my sass.

Let me be a full on orchestra,
then I promise
you'll like me.
You'll jump with me,
into everything
we (I) wanted (us) to be.

13. After a Summer Run

Cold water rain
Trees swaying
Summer heat
Heat mirage
Sweaty forehead
Converse feet
Music treat
jumping beat
Smoothie swallow
Spaghetti straps
caterpillar and bumblebee
Sunny dreams
Ice cream
Smiling with teeth
Me
Free

14. Insecurity Sea

Stop staring at the sea
hoping all your insecurities
will swim away with the mermaids.

15. Adaptation from r.h. Sin's, "she's strong but she's tired"

"his ghost lives in her tears"
-r.h. Sin

His ghost lives in her tears
and tears have built a lifeboat—
surprisingly strong.

This soul
less
ghost.
A lost twin.

Every time she looks at her reflection
she has to cry, just to
see him one last time.

No matter the things he did,
no reason to hate the dead.

16. Build a Boat Dream an Airplane

If your ocean is too deep
and you don't know how to swim
breakdown!
Your breakdown will cut enough wood
for you to build a boat.
If your breakdown isn't intense enough,
close your eyes,
instead,
dream of an airplane.
Ah to fly away
fly away.
Air out your thoughts,
your sadness will wash you onto another shore anyways.

17. Too Something

"Too smart for the jocks"
"Too stupid for the nerds"
"Too plain for the artists"
"Too ugly for the populars"

I think I'll hang with my rabbit.
She thinks I'm just fine.

18. I'd Like To

For my husband, written after one month of dating when
I knew you were the "one."

I'd like to

I'd like to do so many things to you
with you
next to you.

I'd like to run with you
not run away with you but run next to you
hear your gentle breathing interrupted by runners cough
through giant winding trees, bleeding life into our
calloused feet
with each step.
Sun patches shining down on us through green leathery
leaves
your golden olive kaleidoscope eyes
catching my face and tanning me from the
inside out.

Our piano footsteps reaching the dirt
like a melody i've never heard before
I would listen to it over and over again.

Arch beyond arch of everlasting branches
squirrels searching for methodic kisses
I feel like I'm drinking atmospheric coffee.

I want to fly above us and watch how good we feel
no tire, legs fleeing from insignificance—freeing.

Opening into a sapphire scene,
I can feel the heat from your arms,
your runnning shorts,
smells of honey and natural cologne.

I'd like to run with you
not run away from you but run next to you.

I'd like to look into you
to watch your mouth reveal your uplifting smile
lips moving so lightly with each exhale.

There is something so delicious about how you move
while you speak
I can't help but imagine myself floating in and out of you
an open-windowed room with white dancing curtains,
a breeze winding up tendrils of satin fabric.

You're looking at me with such calm, though I see a

sadness
like a man looks at the sea after burying his mother
he can feel her and the world is so big and so vast
without her,
she must be there with him somehow.

I'd like to curl you in my arms
feel the throb of the weight of you lifting into my biceps
rep after rep
breath after breath
my face scrunching from the strength I'm emitting for
you
my muscles twitching for you,
again,
to get so tired: feels so good.

I can't help but want to throw you up in the air
look around to see if "Strongman" is watching then
catch you into me,
like furrowing foxes huddled into red fiery fur.
Though I was the one lifting,
your vascular hands hold me up
the mirror of water fading away from us now
our feet hitting the ground
continuing down the path,
all I can feel is you.

I hope to show you all the intricies to my mind,
and I want to learn yours,
a memorized map of the Grand Canyon,
I want to pleasantly wear you down,
like the rock erosions,
red
dust
covering our eventual old bones.

Me and you, we will run until we cannot.

19. Let Go

Don't let a career become who you are.

Life is so much more.

Work is a part of life, it should not be your life.

Go home and kiss your dog,
your partner,
hug your friend,
your mother and father.

Lay in the sun and feel yourself burning,
the tan will remind you that life is so much more than
sitting in a cubicle more than 40 hours
a week.

The trees should be reminders to let go
they let go of their leaves every fall
and in spring bud new memories.

Take a drink of water,
and let go,
the ones you love will not be here forever,
and neither will you.

20. Water Isolation

Water isolation:
an ocean
a lake
a river
a stream
a pond
in a pool
in a bucket
in a glass
on a leaf
in a tube
in a tear,
and for all of the reasons you cry

just isolated water
each contains a story untold,
each a silent sonnet,
dropped in the well of solitude,
and for all of the silence,
you weep.

21. Eza

Always hungry
searching for love.
A badger hunter at heart,
a dachshund at sight.

With every wag and playful leap,
you fill the silence with barks,
your red coat glistening in the sunlight.